To my friend
& "adopted mom"
God bless
you in your
new apartment.
Love,
Sandy
aug 2003

The language of friendship is not words, but meanings. It is an intelligence above language.

– Henry David Thoreau

Thoughts of FRIENDSHIP

Edited by
Susan Polis Schutz

Blue Mountain Press ®

Boulder, Colorado

Library of Congress Catalog Card Number: 99-15441
ISBN: 0-88396-518-6

ACKNOWLEDGMENTS appear on page 64.

design on book cover is registered in the U.S. Patent and Trademark Office.

Manufactured in the United States of America
First Printing: May 1999

This book is printed on recycled paper.

Library of Congress Cataloging-in-Publication Data

Thoughts of friendship / edited by Susan Polis Schutz.
   p. cm.
  ISBN 0-88396-518-6 (alk. paper)
  1. Friendship Quotations, maxims, etc.   I. Schutz, Susan Polis.
PN6084.F8T46 1999
177'.62--dc21   99-15441
                                          CIP

Blue Mountain Press INC.

P.O. Box 4549, Boulder, Colorado 80306

Table of Contents

Friends

Friends are very special people who accept
each other with an unconditional caring. They

Recognize each other's talents and faults and
acknowledge them without judgment.

They are Incapable of turning away when times
are tough and life's problems seem hard to bear.

Instead, they Encourage each other so they can
enjoy the good times and find strength to endure the

bad times. They're Never afraid to say what
they feel and can be honest without causing

hurt or pain. They can Depend on each other
because they have the kind of trust

that allows them to Share the best and worst
of their lives with laughter and without fear.

You are one of these special people,
and I'm glad you are my friend.

— Andrea L. Hines

It is chance that makes brothers
but hearts that make friends.

– Von Geibel

The greatest of delights
and the best of joys
is to know that
people like to
be with you,
and to know that
you like to be
close to them.

– Maxim Gorky

To be true friends,
you must be
sure of one another.

– Leo Tolstoy

The world is so empty if one thinks only of mountains, rivers, and cities; but to know someone who thinks and feels with us, and who, though distant is close to us in spirit, this makes the earth for us an inhabited garden.

– Johann Wolfgang von Goethe

Don't walk in front of me
   I may not follow
Don't walk behind me
   I may not lead
Walk beside me
And just be my friend.

– Albert Camus

We cannot tell the precise moment when friendship is formed. As in filling a vessel drop by drop, there is at last a drop which makes it run over; so in a series of kindnesses there is at last one which makes the heart run over.

— Samuel Johnson

All men have their frailties, and whoever looks for a friend without imperfections will never find what he seeks.

So long as we love, we serve. So long as we are loved by others, I would almost say we are indispensable; and no man is useless while he has a friend.

We are all travellers in the wilderness of this world, and the best that we find in our travels is an honest friend.

— Robert Louis Stevenson

Friends are not only together
when they are side by side,
even one who is far away...
is still in our thoughts.

— Ludwig van Beethoven

The bird a nest,
the spider a web,
man friendship.

William Blake

When I have opened my heart to a friend,
I am more myself than ever.

— Thomas Moore

The peace of the world will in the end
depend upon our capacity for friendship
and willingness to use it.

— Bertha Conde

Friends Are
Special Treasures

Friends enlarge our world. They make us feel important and more secure in life. Friends work together. They create magic together. They help each other. They get busy, but they keep each other in the forefront of their minds and in the recesses of their hearts. Even when they're apart, friends hear each other's thoughts. Their influence on each other makes a lasting impression.

Friends cross all barriers of race, creed, age, gender, and country to connect only with the heart and spirit, which have no walls. Sometimes they don't even know it when they say the right words at just the right time. Sometimes friends <u>feel</u> <u>like</u> family. Sometimes they <u>are</u> family.

The soul hungers for friendship, someone to associate with, to compare stories with, to go places with, and to call on the phone. We keep the gift and get the blessing of friendship by passing it on to others in this give-and-take world. Thank you for this gift. What a blessing you've been to me!

— Donna Fargo

What Is a Friend?

What is a friend? I will tell you ⤳ It
is a person with whom you dare to be
yourself ⤳ Your soul can be naked with
him ⤳ He seems to ask of you to put
on nothing, only to be what you are ⤳
He does not want you to be better or
worse ⤳ When you are with him, you
feel as a prisoner feels who has been
declared innocent ⤳ You do not have to
be on your guard ⤳ You can say what
you think, so long as it is genuinely you ⤳
He understands those contradictions in
your nature that lead others to misjudge
you ⤳ With him you breathe freely ⤳
You can avow your little vanities and
envies and hates and vicious sparks, your
meannesses and absurdities and, in opening
them up to him, they are lost, dissolved
on the white ocean of his loyalty ⤳

He understands ⌁ You do not have to be careful ⌁ You can abuse him, neglect him, tolerate him ⌁ Best of all, you can keep still with him ⌁ It makes no matter ⌁ He likes you – he is like fire that purges to the bone ⌁ He understands ⌁ He understands ⌁ You can weep with him, sing with him, laugh with him, pray with him ⌁ Through it all – and underneath – he sees, knows and loves you ⌁ A friend? What is a friend? Just one, I repeat, with whom you dare to be yourself ⌁

– C. Raymond Beran

The only way to have a friend
is to be one.

A friend may well be reckoned
the masterpiece of nature.

A friend is a person with whom I may
be sincere. Before him, I may think aloud.

– Ralph Waldo Emerson

A true friend is somebody who can make us do what we can.

God evidently does not intend us all to be rich, or powerful, or great, but He does intend us all to be friends.

— Ralph Waldo Emerson

There are plenty of acquaintances in the world, but very few real friends.

You can hardly make a friend in a year, but you can lose one in an hour.

– Chinese Proverbs

Have no friends not equal to yourself.

There are three friendships which are advantageous, and three which are injurious ⬥ Friendship with the upright; friendship with the sincere; and friendship with the man of much observation; these are advantageous ⬥ Friendship with the man of specious airs; friendship with the insinuatingly soft; and friendship with the glib-tongued; these are injurious.

— Confucius

'Though I am different from you,
We were born involved in one another.

— Tau Ch'ien

A faithful friend is a sturdy shelter
He that has found one
Has found a treasure.

— Ecclesiasticus 6:14

Love your neighbor as yourself.

— Leviticus 19:18 (NKJV)

A faithful friend
is the medicine of life.

— Ecclesiasticus 6:16

A friendless man is like a left hand without a right.

— Hebrew Proverb

Two are better than one, because they have a good reward for their labor. For if they fall, one will lift up his companion. But woe to him who is alone when he falls, for he has no one to help him up.... Though one may be overpowered by another, two can withstand him. And a threefold cord is not quickly broken.

— Ecclesiastes 4:9-10, 12 (NKJV)

A friend is one
to whom one may pour
out all the contents
of one's heart,
chaff and grain together
knowing that the
gentlest of hands
will take and sift it,
keep what is worth keeping
and with a breath of kindness
blow the rest away.

– Arabian Proverb

True friendship between two people is infinite and immortal.

Friendship is, strictly speaking, reciprocal benevolence, which inclines each party to be solicitous for the welfare of the other as for his own. The equality of affection is created and preserved by a similarity of disposition and manners.

— Plato

He who throws away a friend is as bad as he who throws away his life.

— Sophocles

Instead of herds of oxen, endeavor to assemble flocks of friends about your house.

— Epictetus

One of the most beautiful qualities of true friendship is to understand and to be understood.

— Seneca

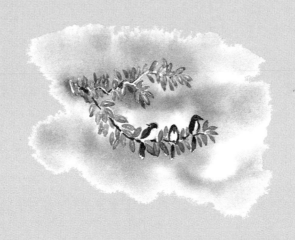

If a man could mount to Heaven and survey the mighty universe, his admiration of its beauties would be much diminished unless he had a friend to share in his pleasure.

Friendship renders prosperity more brilliant, while it lightens adversity by sharing it and making its burden common.

Never injure a friend, even in jest.

— Cicero

A true friend unbosoms freely, advises justly, assists readily, adventures boldly, takes all patiently, defends courageously, and continues a friend unchangeably.

— William Penn

Instead of a gem, or even a flower, we should cast the gift of a loving thought into the heart of a friend, that would be giving as the angels give.

— George MacDonald

As gold more splendid from the fire appears;
Thus friendship brightens by length of years.

— Thomas Carlyle

A Best Friend...

Someone who is concerned with everything
you do ⋇ someone to call upon during
good and bad times ⋇ someone who
understands whatever you do ⋇ someone
who tells you the truth about yourself ⋇
someone who knows what you are going
through at all times ⋇ someone who does
not compete with you ⋇ someone who is
genuinely happy for you when things go
well ⋇ someone who tries to cheer you up
when things don't go well ⋇ someone who
is an extension of yourself without which you
are not complete ⋇
      My best friend is you

                      — Susan Polis Schutz

My Definition of a Friend Is You

A friend is like a sister you never had, a brother you always wanted, a companion you always hoped you'd find. A friend can feel like sunshine when there's too much rain in your life, light when there is darkness, and food that nourishes the landscape of your soul. Having a friend can be pure vision to someone without direction and hope to someone in despair. A friend is someone who goes the extra mile with you and helps you turn the page and will be there until you find an answer to your prayer. When you find a friend, you feel as though you have found a personal treasure and been granted a special blessing.

A friend is someone you share concerns with, from failures to triumphs, through the losing streaks, the dry periods, and the lucky breaks. A friend is someone who provides an anchor when you need balance, won't sink in fear when you are challenged, but will believe with you that you can reach your goal. Friends laugh with you and cry with you. They listen and understand. They accept you without judgment and condition, and they love you just because. When your life gets messy or you're not on top, a friend won't turn away or trade you in for someone more useful or newsworthy or beautiful. Unlike someone who can see a need but remain unmoved by it, a friend is sensitive to your desires and your perceived needs, wants the best for you, whatever that is, and is available to listen, to talk, or to do whatever will help you most. A friend is there for you. Always.

A friend suggests, but does not demand, lets you keep your opinions to yourself or share them, never insists that you agree, but lets you know that your friendship will survive if there ever is disagreement. A friend doesn't want to know things about you that you don't willingly want to share. When you need to move a mountain or just get up some little hill, a friend is your helper, your advocate, someone who's on your side and won't condemn or betray you. On the contrary, a friend accepts you and celebrates your uniqueness.

A friend is there to offer you, not just superficial support, but also the important things, like shelter if you need it, food if you're hungry, and understanding when you could use it most.

Friends will be there when you're all dressed up, to celebrate your accomplishments, but a true friend also is not afraid to hug you if you're down and dirty and it seems like you have nothing much to be proud of. A friend is more interested in the matters of your heart and the well-being of your soul than your material possessions or your appearance to others. There is no such thing as tough love to a friend, for a friend knows it is your level of awareness and not games or manipulation, restrictions or conditions, that will change you, if you need changing. With open arms and acceptance, friends inspire one another to excel and succeed or just move on, and the behavior of a friend must be pure and simple unconditional love in order to educate the heart.

A friend loves you just the way you are, imperfections and all. Friends won't try to change you. They know changing you is your business. Having just one friend can make life more beautiful and help you stay aware of its sacredness. Friends are essential to your emotional survival; they walk beside you when you need company, they stay quiet when you just need to talk, and they delight you when you're short on joy. They know your address, they know your number by heart, and they're aware of your dreams. They're often on your prayer list because they mean so much to you. When the going would be tougher alone, friends make you feel less alienated; they make you feel special. They make you feel that you matter, that you belong. Friends are the people you spend your time with and share your heart space with, because you want to, not because you have to. They're very important. When you have good friends in your life, you are so lucky. I just wanted you to know that you are all these things to me, and my definition of a friend is you.

— Donna Fargo

There are friends... whom we can confide
in without fear of disappointment; who, we
are sure, will never fail us... who always
have healing tenderness for the hurt of our
heart, comfort for our sorrow, and cheer
for our discouragement.

To become another's friend in the true sense
is to take the other into such close living
fellowship that his life and ours are knit
together as one. It is far more than a
pleasant companionship in bright, sunny
hours. A true friendship is entirely unselfish;
it loves not for what it may receive, but for
what it may give.

— J. R. Miller

Having you for a friend
Is like walking through
A field of wildflowers
And not wanting to pick any.
Just knowing that you're there
Makes a bouquet within my heart.

— Ashley Warner

People who have warm friends are healthier and happier than those who have none. A single real friend is a treasure worth more than gold or precious stones. Money can buy many things, good and evil. All the wealth of the world could not buy you a friend or pay you for the loss of one.

— C. D. Prentice

Friends,
no matter how far separated,
will grow
in love
and sympathy
and nearness
to each other.

— Bertha Conde

You know that however much time
passes without your hearing
from me, there is not a day
that does not in some way or other
bring me nearer to you
or remind me
of your friendship.

— Felix Mendelssohn

Friendship – Like music heard on the waters,
Like pines when the wind passeth by,
Like pearls in the depths of the ocean,
Like stars that enamel the sky,
Like June and the odor of roses,
Like dew and the freshness of morn,
Like sunshine that kisseth the clover,
Like tassels of silk on the corn,
Like mountains that arch the blue heavens,
Like clouds when the sun dippeth low,
Like songs of the bird in the forest,
Like brooks where the sweet waters flow,
Like dreams of Arcadian pleasures,
Like colors that gratefully blend,
Like everything breathing of kindness –
Like these is the love of a friend.

– A. P. Stanley

Each of us yearns for a heart
    that beats in unison with our own;
for an ear to which we can
pour out our confidences and troubles,
for a hand we can safely grasp,
for an arm we can always lean on.

But it is not only when difficulties arise
that we know the value of a trusted friend;
but even in our most bright and happy hours,
we feel that joys
    have not half their sweetness
unless we have a companion
    to share them with us.
Whether our dwelling be a
    castle or a cabin,
our trials will be lighter
and our comforts will be richer
if we have a true friend.

— Thain Davidson

I cherish my friends,
for I know that
of all things
granted us...
none is greater
or better
than friendship.

— Pietro Aretino
1537 A.D.

Friendship involves the sharing of the selves.
And one of the greatest aspects, certainly,
of love is joy in personal life.
Each friend must be able to give that joy
and to enter into it...
The very idea of a worthy friendship
implies that the friends need
and desire each other
and so are continuously receptive
and eager for the other's gift.

— Henry Churchill King

Friends are the leaves
of the tree of life.

— George Meredith

A friend is like a star that guides the
way, near and far.

— Catherine Plumb

None of us deserves to be as well
thought of by our friends as we are; but
the beauty of it is, that real friendship
knows us best after all, because it sees in
us our best aim, endeavor, and possibilities,
and lets our failures and imperfections pass
by and be forgotten.

— Lucy Larcom

Oh, for the love of a friend... whose voice and touch will rainbow sorrows and diamond tears, making of them gems of rarest joy; one who forgives all my shortcomings ere asked to do so... one whose ship will cast anchor and throw out the life line of hope when storms are near; one who forgives in me all that I can forgive in myself.

Oh, for the love of a friend... who can be made the sacred trustee of my heart; one who is more to me than the closest relative; one whose very name is so sacred that I want to whisper it softly; one who lingers near my door in times of distress, and stretches out a hand... and who says little but feels largely; one whose very glance radiates tenderness, sympathy, and loving kindness... and who penetrates the very soul of me.

— Mae Lawson

I have always seen my life
as a journey on a road
to tomorrow.
There have been hills and valleys
and turns here and there
that have filled my life with
all kinds of challenges and changes.
But I made it through those times,
because there were always
special friends I met
along the way.

My special friends
are the ones who
have walked beside me,
comforting my spirit or
holding my hand
when I needed it the most.
They were friends who
loved my smiles
and were not afraid of my tears.
They were true friends
who really cared about me.
Those friends are forever;
they are cherished and loved
more than they'll ever know.

— Deanna Beisser

There's a Rainbow
Inside You, My Friend

Its colors arc across the sky
    of your soul,
brimming with life, with hope,
    with love.
It's that inner light that sparkles
    from your eyes, your smile,
        your heart.
You brighten the world
with your caring, your compassion,
    your boundless energy,
        your unquenchable spirit.
What lies within you
    is your greatest gift.
The more you share,
    the more you have to give.
That is your miracle.
That is why you are such a blessing
    to me and to all whose lives
        you touch.
                    — Lynda La Rocca

If a man does not make new acquaintances, as he advances through life, he will soon find himself left alone. A man should keep his friendship in constant repair.

— Samuel Johnson

We can never replace a friend. When a man is fortunate enough to have several, he finds they are all different. No one has double in friendship.

— Johann Friedrich von Schiller

True friendship is of royal lineage. It is of the same kith and breeding as loyalty and self-forgetting devotion and proceeds upon a higher principle even than they. For loyalty may be blind, and friendship must not be; devotion may sacrifice principles of right choice which friendship must guard with an excellent and watchful care.... The object of love is to serve, not to win.

— Woodrow Wilson

Life is sweet because of the
    friends we have made
And the things which in common
    we share;
We want to live on, not because
    of ourselves,
But because of the ones who
    would care.
It's living and doing for
    somebody else
On that all of life's splendor
    depends,
And the joy of it all, when we
    count it all up,
Is found in the making of friends.

                    – Anonymous

I would not live without the love of
my friends.

                    – John Keats

True Friends

There are many people
that we meet in our lives
but only a very few
will make a lasting impression
on our minds and hearts
It is these people that we will
think of often
and who will always remain
important to us
as true friends

— Susan Polis Schutz

To have a friend is to have one of the
sweetest gifts; to be a friend is to experience
a solemn and tender education of soul from
day to day. A friend remembers us when we
have forgotten ourselves. A friend may praise
us and we are not embarrassed. He takes
loving heed of our work, our health, our
aims, our plans. He may rebuke us and we
are not angry. If he is silent, we understand.
It takes a great soul to be a friend…. One
must forgive much, forget much, forbear
much. It costs time, affection, strength,
patience, love. Sometimes a man must lay
down his life for his friends. There is no true
friendship without self-sacrifice. We will be
slow to make friends, but having once made
them, neither life nor death, misunderstanding,
distance nor doubt must ever come between.

– Anonymous

i am so glad and very
merely my fourth will cure
the laziest self of weary
the hugest sea of shore

so far your nearness reaches
a lucky fifth of you
turns people into eachs
and cowards into grow

our can'ts were born to happen
our mosts have died in more
our twentieth will open
wide a wide open door

we are so both and oneful
night cannot be so sky
sky cannot be so sunful
i am through you so i

— E. E. Cummings

The Arrow and the Song

I shot an arrow into the air,
It fell to earth, I knew not where;
For, so swiftly it flew, the sight
Could not follow it in its flight.

I breathed a song into the air,
It fell to earth, I knew not where;
For who has sight so keen and strong,
That it can follow the flight of song?

Long, long afterward, in an oak
I found the arrow, still unbroke;
And the song, from beginning to end,
I found again in the heart of a friend.

— Henry Wadsworth Longfellow

Let us be what we are and speak
what we think and in all things
keep ourselves loyal to truth and the
sacred professions of friendship.

— Henry Wadsworth Longfellow

A slender acquaintance with the world
must convince every man that actions, not
words, are the true criterion of the
attachment of friends; and that the most
liberal profession of good-will is very far
from being the surest mark of it.

— George Washington

There Is No Friend like
an Old Friend

There is no friend like an old friend
Who has shared our morning days.
No greeting like his welcome,
No homage like his praise.

— Oliver Wendell Holmes

The better part of one's life
consists of his friendships.

— Abraham Lincoln

New Friends and Old Friends

Make new friends, but keep the old;
Those are silver, these are gold.
New-made friendships, like new wine,
Age will mellow and refine.
Friendships that have stood the test
Time and change — are surely best;
Brow may wrinkle, hair grow gray;
Friendship never knows decay.
For 'mid old friends, tried and true,
Once more we reach and youth renew
But old friends, alas! may die;
New friends must their place supply.
Cherish friendships in your breast
New is good, but old is best;
Make new friends, but keep the old;
Those are silver, these are gold.

— Joseph Parry

The more we love, the better we are; and the greater our friendships are, the dearer we are to God.

By friendship you mean the greatest love, the greatest usefulness, the most open communication, the noblest sufferings, the severest truth, the heartiest counsel, and the greatest union of minds of which brave men and women are capable.

– Jeremy Taylor

Take Time

Take time for friendship when you can.
The hours fly swiftly, and the need
That presses on your fellowman
May fade away at equal speed
And you may sigh before the end
That you have failed to play the friend.

Not all life's pride is born of fame;
Not all the joy from work is won.
Too late we hang our heads in shame,
Remembering good we could have done;
Too late we wish that we had stayed
To comfort those who called for aid.

Take time to do the little things
Which leave the satisfactory thought,
When other joys have taken wings,
That we have labored as we ought;
That in a world where all contend,
We often stopped to be a friend.

— Edgar A. Guest

I Saw in Louisiana
a Live-Oak Growing

I saw in Louisiana a live-oak growing,
All alone stood it and the moss hung down
    from the branches,
Without any companion it grew there uttering
    joyous leaves of dark green,
And its look, rude, unbending, lusty, made me
    think of myself,
But I wonder'd how it could utter joyous leaves
    standing alone there without its friend near,
    for I knew I could not,
And I broke off a twig with a certain number of
    leaves upon it, and twined around it a little moss,
And brought it away, and I have placed it in sight
    in my room,
It is not needed to remind me as of my own
    dear friends,
(For I believe lately I think of little else than of them,)
Yet it remains to me a curious token, it makes me
    think of manly love;
For all that, and though the live-oak glistens there
    in Louisiana solitary in a wide flat space,
Uttering joyous leaves all its life without a friend
    a lover near,
I know very well I could not.

                        – Walt Whitman

Blessed are they who have the gift of making friends, for it is one of God's best gifts. It involves many things, but above all, the power of going out of one's self, and appreciating whatever is noble and loving in another.

If you have a friend worth loving,
Love him, yes, and let him know
That you love him ere life's evening
Tinge his brow with sunset glow;
Why should good words ne'er be said
Of a friend till he is dead?

– Thomas Hughes

You know how I feel
You listen to how I think
You understand...
You're
my
friend

There is no need for an outpouring
of words to explain oneself to a friend
Friends understand each other's thoughts
even before they are spoken

— Susan Polis Schutz

I haven't seen you in a while
yet I often imagine
all your expressions

I haven't spoken to you recently
but many times
I hear your thoughts

Good friends must not always be together
It is the feeling of oneness when distant
that proves a lasting friendship

— Susan Polis Schutz

I Love You

I love you,
Not only for what you are
But for what I am
When I am with you.

I love you
Not only for what
You have made of yourself
But for what
You are making of me.

I love you
For the part of me
That you bring out;
I love you
For putting your hand
Into my heaped-up heart
And passing over
All the foolish, weak things
That you can't help
Dimly seeing there,
And for drawing out
Into the light
All the beautiful belongings
That no one else had looked
Quite far enough to find.

I love you because you
Are helping me to make
Of the lumber of my life
Not a tavern
But a temple;
Out of works
Of my every day
Not a reproach
But a song.

I love you
Because you have done
More than any creed
Could have done
To make me good,
And more than any fate
Could have done
To make me happy.

You have done it
Without a touch,
Without a word,
Without a sign.

You have done it
By being yourself.
Perhaps that is what
Being a friend means,
After all.

— Roy Croft

What do we live for, if it is not
to make life less difficult to others.

— George Eliot

I have perceived that to be with
those I like is enough.

— Walt Whitman

If I can stop one heart from breaking,
I shall not live in vain;
If I can ease one life the aching,
Or cool one pain,
Or help one fainting robin
Unto his nest again,
I shall not live in vain.

— Emily Dickinson

If we build on a sure foundation in
friendship, we must love our friends for
their sakes rather than for our own.

— Charlotte Brontë

As I love nature, as I love singing birds,
and gleaming stubble, and flowing rivers, and
morning and evening, and summer and winter,
I love thee my friend.

We do not wish for friends to feed and
clothe our bodies – neighbors are kind
enough for that – but to do the like office
for our spirits.

Think of the importance of friendship in
the education of men. It will make a man
honest; it will make him a hero; it will
make him a saint. It is the state of the just
dealing with the just, the magnanimous
with the magnanimous, the sincere with the
sincere, man with man.

– Henry David Thoreau

The most I can do for my friend
is simply to be his friend.

Be true to your word,
your work, and your friend.

The language of friendship is not
words, but meanings. It is an
intelligence above language.

– Henry David Thoreau

True Friendship
Has Many Ingredients

True friendship isn't seen
    with the eyes;
it's felt with the heart
when there is trust,
    understanding, secrets,
loyalty, and sharing.
Friendship is a feeling
    rarely found in life,
but when it is found
it has a profound impact
    on one's well-being,
strength, and character.

A true friendship does not need
    elaborate gifts
or spectacular events
in order to be valuable or valued.

To ensure long-lasting quality
    and satisfaction,
a friendship only needs
    certain key ingredients:
undying loyalty,
unmatched understanding,
unsurpassed trust,
deep and soulful secrets,
and endless sharing.
These ingredients, mixed with
personality and a sense of humor,
can make friendship
last a lifetime.

— Sonya Williams

ACKNOWLEDGMENTS

We gratefully acknowledge the permission granted by the following authors, publishers, and authors' representatives to reprint poems or excerpts from their publications.

PrimaDonna Entertainment Corporation for "Friends Are Special Treasures," by Donna Fargo. Copyright © 1996 by PrimaDonna Entertainment Corporation. And for "My Definition of a Friend Is You," by Donna Fargo. Copyright © 1999 by PrimaDonna Entertainment Corporation. All rights reserved. Reprinted by permission.

HarperCollins Publishers, Inc. for "When I have opened my heart..." from SOUL MATES by Thomas Moore. Copyright © 1994 by Thomas Moore. All rights reserved. Reprinted by permission.

Ashley Warner for "Having you for a friend...." Copyright © 1999 by Ashley Warner. All rights reserved. Reprinted by permission.

Lynda La Rocca for "There's a Rainbow Inside You, My Friend." Copyright © 1999 by Lynda La Rocca. All rights reserved. Reprinted by permission.

Liveright Publishing Corporation for "I am so glad and very," copyright © 1940, 1968, 1991 by the Trustees for the E. E. Cummings Trust, from COMPLETE POEMS 1904-1962 by E. E. Cummings, edited by George J. Firmage. All rights reserved. Reprinted by permission.

Regnery Publishing, Inc. for "Take Time" from COLLECTED VERSE by Edgar A. Guest. Copyright © 1934 by Regnery Publishing. All rights reserved. Reprinted by special permission of Regnery Publishing, Inc., Washington, D.C.

A careful effort has been made to trace the ownership of poems and excerpts used in this anthology in order to obtain permission to reprint copyrighted materials and give proper credit to the copyright owners. If any error or omission has occurred, it is completely inadvertent, and we would like to make corrections in future editions provided that written notification is made to the publisher:

BLUE MOUNTAIN PRESS, INC., P.O. Box 4549, Boulder, Colorado 80306.